AUNT CORA'S COMPLETE CAT CATALOGUE

AUNT CORA'S COMPLETE CAT CATALOGUE

ARTHUR HOWARD & CHUCK ORTLEB

St. Martin's Press
New York

Library of Congress Cataloging in Publication Data
Ortleb, Charles.
    Aunt Cora's complete cat catalogue.
    1. Cats—Caricatures and cartoons. 2. American wit
and humor, Pictorial. I. Howard, Arthur. II. Title.
NC1429.0616A4   1985   741.5'973   84-22311
ISBN 0-312-06080-7 (pbk.)

First Edition
10 9 8 7 6 5 4 3 2 1

Dear Cat Owner:

My grandmother, Grandma Cora, founded our company in 1879 with the idea of vastly improving the lot of the American cat. Back in those days, Grandma's little company manufactured magic elixirs to cure distemper and Indian cat fever, and balms to stimulate fur growth. But it was Ye Olde Scratching Post that really put Grandma Cora on the map.

Over the years, Grandma Cora, Great-Aunt Cora, Cousin Cora, and sister-in-law Cora have developed the most revered and varied mail-order empire in the world for cats and cat owners who have money to burn.

You see, Grandma Cora had a simple philosophy: "Pamper the cat and no matter the cost!" Grandma Cora wanted to put a little happy face on every cat in America. (Our 1942 catalog featured our first line of cosmetic smiles that could be painted on Kitty's face! We've sure come a long way. This year, our Martha Raye dentures give every cat that special show-biz smile.)

Our factory, offices, and kitchens employ over 900 people, and all of them are named Cora—even the men. Their devotion to the cat and the cat owner is intense and abiding. No detail is overlooked; our quality control is the best. Every year, for example, we safety-test all of our products on dogs (I don't believe in endangering *our* friends), and any product that causes the death of more than fifty dogs is immediately withdrawn from the market.

Aunt Cora is a name that has come to mean "I trust you with my cat" to thousands of you.

Because I'll never let a kitty down.

Felinitously,
Aunt Cora
President, Chairman of the Board, Mother of Us All

THE CASTRO CONVERTIBLE LITTER BOX

Here's another Aunt Cora solution to the problems of urban overcrowding, tight apartments . . . and scattered litter. The Castro Convertible Litter Box also solves the dilemma of how to conceal the unsightly *boîte de toilette* from your guests. When they're visiting your lovely home, **they won't even know they're sitting on it.** Kitty need only perch behind the left-hand cushion (see illustration) and the couch flings open into a luxurious litter box, **so large kitty can entertain her own friends.**

CCLB9804
Castro Convertible Litter Box
Navy Canvas $585
Floral Pattern $750
(100% cotton)

SPECIAL!

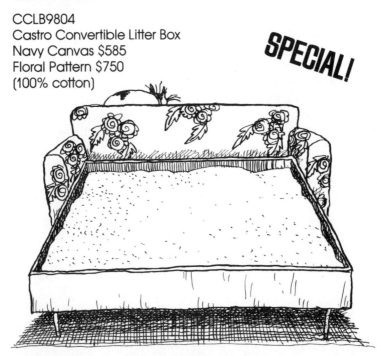

THE MANHATTAN BOHEMIAN BEAN BAG/LITTER LINER/COMFORT STATION*
*as seen in *New York* magazine

Why shouldn't litter areas be decorative? Since Kitty spends so much time attending to her delicate toilette and you spend so much time cleaning up after her, Aunt Cora has developed a Bean Bag Comfort Station **for the casual cat who never knows what apartment he'll find himself in.** Makes Kitty feel at home with the eccentrics in your life. Why should Kitty have to leave the room when you and your friends are discussing the poetry of Jack Kerouac? With the Bean Bag Comfort Station, Kitty will fit right in with the White Wine Spritzer set.

BB38094
The Manhattan
$75
(With Track Lights: $175)

THE QE2 LITTER LINER

This is one of Aunt Cora's personal favorites—perfect for the cat who's always wanted to travel without leaving home. And if Kitty kicks litter around, it doesn't end up on your bathroom floor: it's simply lost at sea. Kitty just has to leap from the side of the bathtub into her elegant cruise litter box **for truly oceanic relief.** (NOTE: Sorry—our popular Titanic litter box is no longer available.)

QE9800f
QE2 Litter Box
Assembled: $75.00
Kit: $45.00

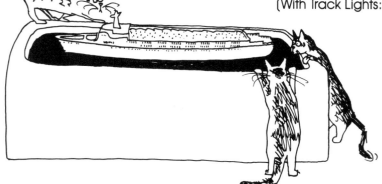

THE LOUIS XVI LITTER BOX

Based on the original used by Louis XVI's favorite cat, before his untimely beheading. Aunt Cora's fussy craftsmen have spared no expense in duplicating every detail of the original. After all, as Aunt Cora says, a cat's life is short—why shouldn't every litter experience be a joy?

FIU0289309843
Louis XVI Litter Box
$12,985
(Allow Two Years for Delivery)

THE LITTER LOFT

The dream answer to the urban nightmare of small apartments. From the same architectural geniuses who gave you loft beds and floating terrariums. Now you can have both litter control and rent control. Make the feline litter experience an elevating one. Kitty just climbs up to her bio-system in the sky. Also a favorite among cats who can throw.

JA 165-64-W68
The Litter Loft
$159.95 (Installation: $1,300.00)

SPECIALIZED KITTY LITTER:
All the Litter That's Fit to Print

This is the perfect solution for cats who like to read while they're in the litter box. Aunt Cora will send you a year's supply of *New York Times* litter (with *all* the crossword puzzles completed by Aunt Cora herself). It's so convenient—all you have to do is tear up as much as you need and read the rest. **Especially recommended for white liberal upper-class cats.**

Specialized Kitty Litter
125 pounds: JUST $50
($325 Shipping and Handling)

NEW!

THE AUNT CORA LITTER PLANS

PLAN A

For one annual fee, Aunt Cora's sister Ma Wisconsin will ship you a weekly supply of the latest litter products. Environmentally safe. We send you a complete month's supply every month with a different unique scent. (Apple, chestnut mint, turkey-gizzard, new-auto, hippie-sweat, pine chip, senior-citizen, cherry, locker room, vanilla, strawberry, doctor's office, and tutti-frutti). **All the scents of a well-rounded feline life.** Your apartment will be a constant odorous surprise to your houseguests.

PHEW714-2G
The Aunt Cora
Litter-of-the-Month Plan
Twelve-Month Supply: $120.00

NOTE: Not recommended for depressed cats.
100 lbs. for $100.00

SAVE!

PLAN B

A revolutionary litter concept! Environmentally sound. **No odors, no fuss, no bother.** Waste disappears forever.

KITTY BIDET (It's Not a Spittoon!)

Does Kitty lick herself *constantly* "down there?" Is this creating complex breath problems? Well, straight from obsessive-compulsive Europe, these Kitty Bidets **for the cat who can never be too clean.** Especially popular among cats who are afraid of sexually transmitted diseases. Perfect for owners who are afraid that guests can tell that "this is a home with a cat" from the moment they enter and take their first whiff. Made of Perma-porcelain,® and compatible with all toilet tank mechanisms. Hose supplied.

KB502749
Kitty Bidet
$250.00
(Specify White, Blue, or Gold)

BACK TO NATURE: THE BASIC LEISURE CAT CARRIER—PORTA-KITTY

Aunt Cora has devised one of the few cat carriers that doesn't cause a disturbing oxygen shortage. Porta-kitty is 100 percent canvas and natural fibers, designed to allow Kitty to see the way bats do, while enjoying the back arch-support pads. (And because Kitty is upside down, she won't struggle so.) Comes with a year's supply of motion-sickness pills. Porta-kitty is **a particular favorite among preppies and young urban professionals on the go.** Just toss Kitty in and you're on your way.

POL58094
Porta-kitty
Beige, Black Handles
Navy, Maroon Handles
Maroon, Navy Handles
$39.95

SPECIAL!

BANG & OLUFSEN STEREO LITTER CENTER

For the owner who wants to create **a unique litter center,** knowing that litter is indeed the center of little Kitty's earth experience. This unusual high-tech stereo litter design is especially programmed to play music whenever Kitty is accurate enough to hit the box. Heat sensitive to Kitty's most private processes. Adjusted to feline hearing. Filled with acoustically refined litter.

28167 K
Bang & Olufsen Litter Box
$995.00 Postpaid

TO ACCOMMODATE THE PENTAGON'S STAR WARS PLANS: THE KITTY SHUTTLE

As a result of over a trillion dollars spent in defense research for our astronauts' pets, Aunt Cora is offering—for a limited time only—the Kitty Shuttle. Kitty floats in an antigravity chamber with all cat-support systems at her convenience. Children love to watch Kitty attack the hundreds of Tender Vittles that float around her chamber with her. Designed for the cat who is bored with the old-fashioned methods of transportation. Also **ideal for use in the New York City subway or on the Los Angeles freeway.**

FL0987
The Kitty Shuttle—While They Last
$270,495.00
(Shipping Included)

THE GHETTO BLASTER

For oppressed minorities on a budget. **Look years younger** as you transport Kitty on city buses. Guarantees safe passage in ethnic areas. Especially recommended for kitties who know how to breakdance. The only carrying case **guaranteed** to get respect from white people's cats.

2853K.
Ghetto Blaster Carrying Case
$49.95
(Tapes $5.95 Extra)

SECURITY MINDED?
THE BULLET-PROOF CARRYING CASE

Perfect for overseas assignments or weekends in New York City. Designed in consultation with top South American dictators. Recommended for U.S. ambassadors, Mafia wives, U.S. military personnel, and retired paranoids. Kitty will be amused to see guns pointed at her and bullets ricocheting into passersby. Also a favorite carrying case for papal cats. **Built to resist small nuclear explosions** in case of a limited nuclear war.

KLMPT 965
Bullet-Proof Carrying Case
$395.00

PRE-STAINED CARPETING

It's Oriental, so it's pre-stained with Chinese food as digested. It can take years for the average cat to stain a carpet artistically. Our research team has used some of the most sophisticated biochemical techniques to duplicate nearly every substance with which Kitty's bio-system can enhance a carpet. From the first day, **kitty will be thrilled** with a carpet that meets all of her visual needs.

FUIDf80
Pre-Stained Carpeting
$8.95 a Yard

ACTUAL SIZE
Note close-up of moo-goo gai pan stain carefully simulated by Aunt Cora's Research Lab.

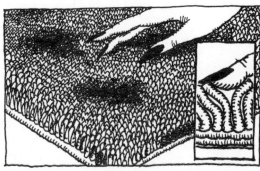

DESK ESCRITOIRE

Escritoire: that upon which one writes, sits, purrs, or chews. This carefully pre-clawed piece of furniture was designed by a gay descendant of Louis XIV (who we all know was a devoted cat lover). Ideal for cats who write highly pretentious cat books. Available in walnut, oak, cherry, or pre-chewed Formica.

DE48093
Desk Escritoire
$1,495
Available in
   Walnut
   Oak
   Cherry
   Formica

A BARGAIN!

PRE-CLAWED LOUNGER

This lounger has been pre-clawed so it will have **that comfy, lived-in look** from the very day it arrives. Kitty doesn't have to waste precious hours giving it that special designer look cats prefer. Also comes with pre-scratched footrest and phony loose strings that lead nowhere, so Kitty can play for hours without unravelling the whole chair.

PCL58943
Pre-Clawed Lounger
$179.95
With Footrest: $200
(Navy, Beige, Orange ONLY)

NEW!

DESIGNER SCRATCHED COUCH

Our designers will carefully ruin a classic couch before Kitty can get her paws on it. There's nothing that Kitty can do to this beautiful piece of furniture that doesn't enhance its look. A matching lamp is also provided. **Save hours of interior decorating heartache** by owning a couch that has been ruined by professionals.

DLS80594
Designer Scratched Couch
(As Illustrated, with Lamp) $1,200
Special Flare-Armed Design: $1,300

Black
Brown
Cream
Gray
_____ Other (Add $600)

MA WISCONSIN'S WATER BED (Only Recommended for De-clawed Cats)

Just put a few goldfish in it and watch Kitty go **wild!** Give Kitty one of the finest nights of sleep ever. Sized perfectly. Kitty can sleep on her own little ocean and dream little amniotic-fluid dreams. Comes complete with Scotch tape repair kit. Easy to fill. (Kitty must be warned not to use it as a backup litter box.)

98764Q
Ma Wisconsin Water Bed
($69.95 Postpaid)

ES-CAT-LATOR

Heart problems? Neuralgia? Arthritis? Psoriasis? Ever think how many lives all that stair-climbing takes off your kitties' lives? Thinking of doing a remake of *The Farmer's Daughter?* This all-electric Es-Cat-Lator was designed **for aristocratic cats** who do not deign to ascend and descend like common house cats. Responds to Kitty's nautical weight. Allows Kitty to do what cats are best at: posing for picture postcards. Comes with motion-sickness bag for cats who are squeamish about height.

27985 M
Es-Cat-Lator
($2,500 Postpaid)

WASHER & DRYER IN ONE

Saves hours of licking. Especially useful in multiple cat dwellings. Just load up the entire family and in minutes they're all clean. This carefully designed solid state dryer is a **favorite among obsessive-compulsive owners.** Just strap Kitty in and special oxygen masks lower themselves over each cat, and Kitty suddenly experiences what it's like to be chained to a rock in the Niagara Falls. An invigorating bathing experience for any cat. Saves on tongue wear and prevents choking on hair balls.

WD14-007-2-13
Washer & Dryer in One
8 Cat Size $995.00
12 Cat Size $1,200.00

FELINE SMOKE ALARM

This is a specially designed safety device for cats who do not respond to the normal sounds of human emergencies. Aunt Cora's technicians have recorded the sounds made by cats **actually trapped** in recent fires (they were, of course, rescued). Kitty will immediately know from the frantic meows that it's time to grab a packet of Tender Vittles and get out. Available in two kinds of recordings (second- and third-degree burn sounds).

00-67432-15
Feline Smoke Alarm
$59.95

THE J. EDGAR HOOVER BATTERY-OPERATED SELF-CLEANING VACUUM WITH ATTACHMENTS

For that especially obsessive-compulsive cat who likes to get into those hard-to-reach places that give Kitty nagging doubts about personal hygiene. Invented by the former FBI director, it comes with every attachment necessary to collect all those sweet little nothings that collect on Kitty's fur and wreak havoc with her impeccable image. Includes three brushes for all genetic variations of felinity. **The J. Edgar Hoover is a hair ball's worst enemy.**

IKJLPN
The J. Edgar Hoover Vacuum
$69.95

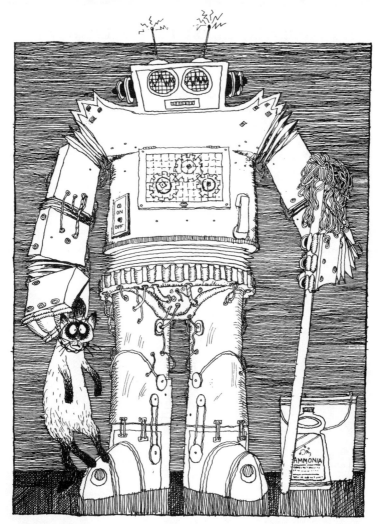

NANNY ROBOT

Thanks to the exceptional design—yes, Aunt Cora had this one made in Japan—you can leave Kitty alone **for months at a time.** Nanny Robot takes care of all Kitty's meals and is programmed to keep the water bowl filled with fresh water at all times. If Kitty scratches any furniture, Nanny Robot de-claws Kitty right on the spot. Operating on 150 D-cell batteries, Nanny Robot has that extra special human touch: stereo speakers in Nanny Robot's chest play the Watergate hearings all day long.

5804-LF
Nanny Robot
$45,000
(Batteries Not Included)

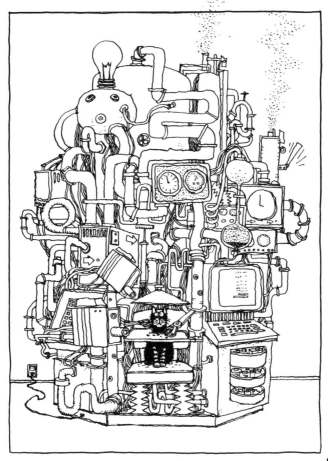

PILL-INJECTING MACHINE

This carefully designed pill-delivery system takes the pain out of getting Kitty to open up and swallow. Complex circuitry and timing mechanisms get that pill around to Kitty. (Kitty's not afraid to enter the delivery system; she'll think she's visiting a factory.) Mechanical arms gently but securely hold Kitty and save your own arms from those **nasty little scratches** that Kitty's pill phobia sometimes leave. The machine is favored by top feline dentists around the country. Just fit Kitty into her **pill-reception position** and watch the machine go to work within thirty minutes. Kitty's unwarranted fears will be overcome as the robot hands gently pry open her mouth and a pneumatic tube is inserted, through which the appropriate medication is propelled by a jet stream into Kitty's bio-system.

PM578934
Pill-Injecting Machine
$1,200 (Including Shipping and Assembly)

FELINE DIET DRINKS

Now Kitty can develop the same neoplasms as Monsieur and Madame! While you've been sipping away on your thirty-two-chemical cola, we've developed an **industrial brew** for your beloved Kitty. Nothing gets Kitty up and moving and really *dealing* with those balls of string and telephone cords like a can of Tabby with breakfast.

9647K Sugar-Free Tabby
9648K Kitty Free
9649K Kitty Lite
One Year's Supply: $498.00
(NOTE: Do Not Store Near a Refrigerator or a Pacemaker)

ALL NEW!

DESIGNER VITTLES

An aristocratic taste treat of surprise meats molded into the shapes
of Kitty's favorite diet items by people who have had years of experience designing jeans and bedspreads. Scrumptious and appetizing
shapes include dead birds, dead squirrels, dead fish, dead ducks,
dead mice, dead chicken, and expensive plants. Smother Kitty in
Godiva vittles tonight.

F84118
Designer Vittles
Twelve-Ounce Fantasy: $55.00

ALICE B. TOKLAS CAT FOOD: HEAVENLY HASH (For Females Only)

This specially formulated cat food is **perfect for woman-identified cats** and those members of the feline population who are owned by drug-damaged members of the Woodstock generation. The ingredients are specially grown in Thailand under the expert tutelage of Buddhist nuns.

F59865
Alice B. Toklas Cat Food
Per Can (45 Grams): $175

EUELL GIBBONS 100% NATURAL CAT FOOD

For the outdoorsy cat who likes a little taste of the real world. A healthy blend of mulch, tree roots, picket-fence slivers, and the entrails of various animals found rotting on the roads surrounding John Denver's home in Colorado.

F32756
Euell Gibbons Cat Food
Twenty-four Cans: $12.95

KITTY COSY

When Kitty's not wanted or is not in use, protect her from dust and crumbs with the Kitty Cosy. Keep Kitty warm while she's thinking of something charming to do. Fits all sizes. Specially designed ventilation system allows Kitty to go on living.

KC48903
Kitty Cosy
SPECIAL! ONLY $15.95
While They Last

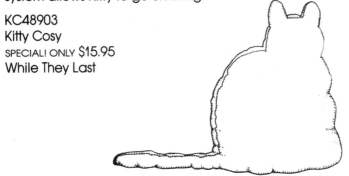

THE TONGUE EXTENDER

For cats who aren't ashamed to make themselves part of the family dinner gathering. Especially recommended for cats who have graduated from assertiveness training classes. This amazing device is the result of years of robotic research on paraplegic cats.

76493 V
The Tongue Extender
(Three Yards of Tongue: $195.00)
(Available in Pink or Coated)

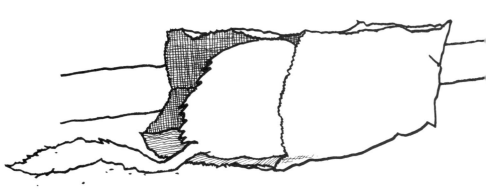

MODULAR/MOBILE ROOM OF KITTY'S OWN

This is the perfect architectural solution for the cat who likes to travel and see new places without being able to leave—ever. Aunt Cora has converted shopping bags into mini-co-ops and mobile homes for Kitty. Disposable and architecturally sound; we provide you with a year's supply of these **trendy paper-bag homes.** Specify whether for indoor or outdoor use.

NP7986-2
Rooms of Kitty's Own
A Complete Supply of Fifteen
Rooms for Just $15

SALE!

KIT KAT BREATH MINTS

Does Kitty smell like she just ate something the cat dragged in—and does she show she knows it by covering her mouth with her paw each time she meows? Do the plants wilt every time Kitty sighs? Are the neighbors constantly reporting a leak the gas company can never find?

   Then Kitty needs **the mint that keeps the social contract intact.** One Kit Kat would even kill odors left in Kitty's mouth by the Andromeda Strain.

PEW7895
Kit Kat Mints
$1.25 for Fifty Mints
$12 Per Dozen Packs

AUNT CORA'S MOUSE-OF-THE-MONTH CLUB

During the first week of every month, you'll find Kitty perched on the windowsill watching for the U.P.S. truck, because that's when we'll be sending Kitty the most unique and delicious mouse products ever devised. Only the plumpest and cleanest mice are used in these products—and only mice that have been killed by cats here in Wisconsin (no traps, poisons, or preservatives).

Kitty will kick off the New Year with tasty flash-frozen Mouse Burgers, which arrive in their own little pita-bread pouches. In February, it's time for Kitty to be transported to Baghdad-By-The-Sea with our special San Francisco Mice-A-Roni, delicately flavored with Catnip — enough to provide Kitty with a week of Pacific breezes. March is time for Aunt Cora's trio of rare and spicy soups: Mouse Chowder, Mouse Gumbo (put a dollop of sour cream on top!), and Mouse Alphabet Soup (all soups are guaranteed to be absolutely boneless). April brings Peking Mouse—a special treat all the way from Chinatown in Manhattan, where this delicacy is actually served in restaurants. Velvety egg noodle is wrapped around tiny morsels of mouse flesh. And Kitty will dance for the hot mustard! May and June it's off to

sunny Greece for a two-month supply of Moussaka—indescribably delicious, and so much more digestable than lamb. July is hot, so it's time for Mice Cream, made only with albino mice. More cool dessert for August: a generous eighteen ounces of Mouse Mousse, a Parisian treat so rich that Kitty should only have it twice a week. That brings us to the autumn favorite, Rat-Tatouie, featuring hickory-smoked rat bellies and seedless tomatoes. In mid-October (if Kitty can wait!), we send our sweet Brandied Mouse Tails, steam cleaned, simmered, and bottled every August by Aunt Cora herself, right along with her brandied peaches. Then, just before Thanksgiving, we send enough sun-dried Mouse Ears to last till well after Christmas. These feathery delights will be a favorite whenever Kitty entertains her holiday guests.

Mouse-of-the-Month Club is *the* ideal Christmas present for every Kitty you know. Put your orders in by November 15, and Kitty will be sampling Mouse Burgers by New Year's Day. (Sorry, no substitutions.)

TKLMFI279797-12
Aunt Cora's Mouse-of-the-Month Club
Annual Membership: $150

TROJAN DUCK

Nothing makes it easier for Kitty to satisfy that craving for duck than these carefully crafted decoys. Specially weighted cork construction allows Kitty to float peacefully and invisibly inside until that murderous moment. Aunt Cora herself likes to take three or four with her when she goes duck hunting, and she brings home **twenty ducks a day.** Purchasers are warned that placing overweight cats in these decoys can lead to personal tragedies.

FD40983
Decoys
$50

CAMOUFLAGED BIRD FEEDER

This ingenious bird feeder is a favorite of every cat and of nine out of ten birds, because nine out of ten birds receive **delicious nutrition** while one out of ten birds becomes delicious nutrition for Kitty. Kitty gets her fresh air while acquiring a taste for the predatory delights of being in the natural state. Ecologically approved by Ralph Nader.

BF48903
Bird Feeder
$39.95

DE-CLAWED MOUSE FOR DE-CLAWED CATS

Aunt Cora believes in a truly fair fight—even when it comes to rodent/ feline skirmishes, so she and her crack research team have genetically engineered a field mouse without claws. Unfortunately, Aunt Cora is still perfecting the little creature (at present, he can only run backward), but by the time you order a litter of six, they'll be ready to outrun Kitty **for hours of fun.** Large ears give the field mouse a slight advantage over Kitty . . . but not for long!

MM4809234
De-clawed Mice
Per Six: $75.00

VETERINARY WALL HANGINGS

Some of the favorite creatures in Kitty's lives: for just $15,000, we'll kill and mount your cat's vet for you. **Nothing gives kitty a stronger sense of security and power** than a dead veterinarian hanging on the wall where Kitty can always see it. Aunt Cora has made a special deal with some of the most discreet members of the Mafia—no one will ever know where it came from.

VT3479-349-28409
Mounted Vet: $15,000
(Specialist: Add $10,000)

WATER-FINDER SYSTEM

For the cat whose water needs are not met by the traditional water bowl, or when the master or mistress is forgetful: the Aunt Cora Water-Finder System leads Kitty to all prominent sources of available H_2O, including cactus plants and underground rivers. Many of our employees actually use this divining rod to find the single Aunt Cora toilet that services our 955 factory workers.

FO47983
Water-Finder System
Birch $29.95
Maple $49.95
Rubber $19.95

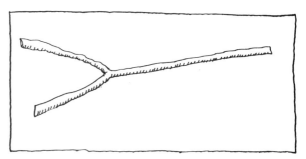

THE AUNT CORA ANSWERING MACHINE AND TAPES

Only works with push-button phones because Aunt Cora knows that Kitty is physically challenged when it comes to operating dial phones and answering machines and can openers. Either you leave the message or Kitty does. Now Kitty doesn't have to miss important calls when she's totally absorbed by that ball of twine. Have your friends spotted an inebriated squirrel on a very low branch—just there for the taking? Why should Kitty miss out on the **opportunity of a lifetime?**

AM58384
Answering Machine
$45.00
(Includes Two Tapes)

PROFESSIONAL COMMERCIAL CLASS

So Kitty's become a television commercial model and actress, but she can't tell the difference between the camera and the plate in front of her? Does Kitty have difficulty achieving enthusiasm for cat food after the fortieth take? Are her eyes dilated like polka dots in the bright studio lights? Is her meow more like a meouch? All these and many more problems are resolved—**or your money back**—at Aunt Cora's Professional Commercial Classes, held for two sessions of three weeks every spring. Yes, the late Morris the Cat was one of Aunt Cora's first students, and before her classes he barely knew how to walk, let alone talk and write. Classes are restricted to ten cats, so **enroll now!**

PCC480
Aunt Cora's Professional
Commercial Classes
Three weeks, April 1–21 or May 1–21,
In Aunt Cora Valley, Wisconsin
$5,000
Applications on Request.

THE L.A. TREATMENT FOR KITTY

Aunt Cora has a special service to offer cats who may feel neglected while their owners are at work or away on vacation. Simply give us the hours and the phone number, and **we'll call Kitty** to tell her what a wonderful cat she is, what an effective mouser, what a comfort to the household, and so forth. We'll **boost Kitty's ego for ten minutes a day (and up)** for a base monthly charge of $40 (plus reversal charges on your telephone bill). **Specify whether a male or female voice** would best reach Kitty, give us Kitty's name, tell us about any special topics to avoid, plug in the phone, and leave the rest to us.

PR101
Public Relations for Kitty
$40/ten minutes/day
$60/eleven minutes/day
etc.
(Reversal Charges not Included)

HOME CAT SCAN

Aunt Cora regularly receives correspondence from inconsolably bereft cat owners who tell her, "If only we'd caught it in time." This breaks Aunt Cora's heart, because it's so **unnecessary to miss regular checkups.** But now, Aunt Cora has made it virtually impossible for cat owners to overlook even the slightest internal disorder. In close cahoots with her twelve-member Cat Oncology and Internist research team, Aunt Cora has developed the Home Cat Scan, which can be installed in any basement or rec room with only a few hundred dollars in extra electricity. Now you can keep a good and regular eye on all of Kitty's internal functions and dysfunctions—painlessly and as easily as watching television. Allow six weeks for installation; maintenance contract and attendant physician optional.

xxx58902
Home Cat Scan $400,000
Maintenance Contract $75,000 Yearly
Physician $750,000 Yearly

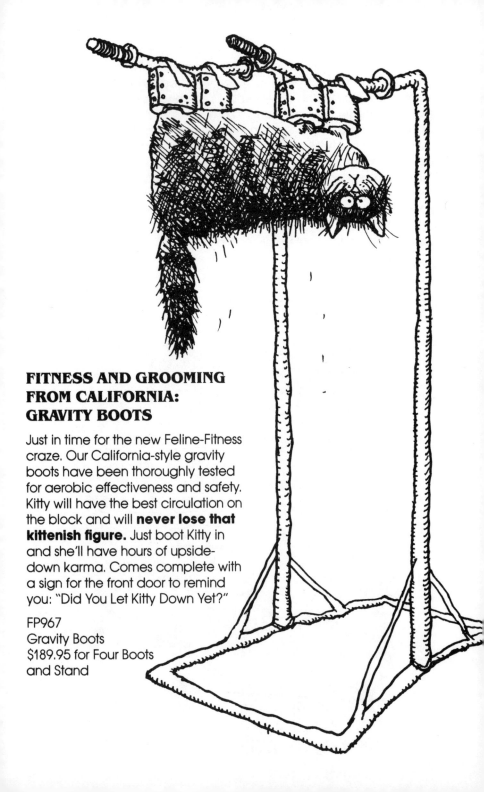

FITNESS AND GROOMING FROM CALIFORNIA: GRAVITY BOOTS

Just in time for the new Feline-Fitness craze. Our California-style gravity boots have been thoroughly tested for aerobic effectiveness and safety. Kitty will have the best circulation on the block and will **never lose that kittenish figure.** Just boot Kitty in and she'll have hours of upside-down karma. Comes complete with a sign for the front door to remind you: "Did You Let Kitty Down Yet?"

FP967
Gravity Boots
$189.95 for Four Boots
and Stand

PRIVATE DISCIPLINARIAN

Remember some of your own problems in learning how to behave correctly and politely in life? Kitty is no different, and what resolved those problems for you will work wonders for her. Aunt Cora retains a staff of thirty septagenarian women who know more about instilling "motivational factors"—primarily guilt in all its forms—than a mother superior. Your cat need not be "wayward" to benefit from Aunt Cora's private disciplinary classes, but if Kitty *is* wayward, we'll send her back a **new, considerate creature** incapable of behaving without regard for the feelings of others. Some of Aunt Cora's methods cannot be described here (they're secret!), but entrust your cat to us and you'll never have to clean her litter box, cover her furniture scratchings, or overfeed her again!

Six to Eight Weeks (Females) $20,000
Thirty Weeks Minimum (Males) $18,000
Travel and Lodging Arrangements Included

A WEEKEND AT A CAT SPA

We fly Kitty to Palm Springs for a week of **exquisite pampering** that only cats of the truly rich have ever experienced. Kitty will dine on only the best meats and fishes. Kitty's claws will be manicured by our own Miss Stiletto Heel. Kitty will be massaged daily by our own famous Bruce of Paris. Kitty will also receive any required special treatment from our group of plastic surgeons from Switzerland: lines around Kitty's eyes and mouth will be infected away with our own special Feline Collagen Treatment. Kitty will be entertained every night by refugee Feline Belly Dancers from Afghanistan. It's like **a week in cat heaven,** and Kitty will return to you refreshed and revitalized.

TWA57094
Cat Spa Special! $3,000
(Double Occupancy: $2,600)

Tending Kitty's every need are:

1. Maitre D' Bruce of Paris
2. Dietician Sarajeva Ricotta Piazza
3. Our resident plastic surgeon and psychoanalyst
4. The upstairs maid
5. Kitty's astrologer
6. Feline manicurist
7. The downstairs maid
8. Chef Cat-ar-Dee
9. Butch the masseur
10, 11, 12, 13: Contented customers

COMPLETE FUR REPLACEMENT

The latest in surgical procedures are applied by the Aunt Cora Fur Transplant team. Our plastic surgeons are flown in from Switzerland and the top medical schools in Grenada and Barbados. Kitty no longer has to suffer the embarrassment of a receding coat. We use a variety of methods, including implants, transplants, and body reductions. Kitty can **even swim** with her new fur replacements. Aunt Cora herself must approve of every replacement, so that Kitty's friends and owners won't ever be able to ask: "Did she or didn't she?"

F48093
Fur Replacement
$1,900 to $3,500
(Varies with Degree of Feline Balding)
Free Consultation in Aunt Cora Valley,
Wisconsin. By Appointment Only.

THE MAMIE EISENHOWER PERMANENT

Especially recommended for the cat who is beginning to look like Mamie Eisenhower on a bad day. Give a little life to that fuzz with a home permanent. Comes complete with curling irons and Krazy Glue setting gel. Also comes with anaesthetic for cats who won't sit still. **Provides hours of curling fun.** Then try to get the phone cord tangled in the new curls. Delights bored owners.

25689Z
The Mamie Permanent
Supplies for Four Perms
$59.95

KITTY VISINE

Do Kitty's eyes get red from staring intently for hours at dust motes in space? Being able to see things in the dark (especially things that aren't there) can exhaust a sensitive pair of eyes—and your cat surely has one of the *most* sensitive. Just put two drops in each eye and Kitty will look as if she just returned from a clinic in Switzerland. Kitty Visine soothes as it clears any sign of eyestrain. Especially recommended for the feminine feline given to long nights out with the neighborhood Tom.

KV-274837
Kitty Visine
Four Ounces:
$9.00

MARTHA RAYE CAT DENTURES

Exchange that boring Cheshire grin for a famous Hollywood smile. Now Kitty can liven up any home with the same look that's seen on the stars of Hollywood and Las Vegas. The first week you have them, everyone will talk about how human Kitty seems. Optional cassette is available containing Martha Raye jokes, which Kitty can play while mouthing the words.

MRCD58098
Martha Raye Cat Dentures
(Uppers, Lowers, Cassette)
$45.00
One Size Fits All!

ARTIFICIAL CLAWS

Get rid of the **needless embarrassment** of clawlessness. Anxiety-prone cats who bite their nails no longer have to worry about being seen in society. These innovative claws are also a favorite among the de-clawed who don't want other cats to know about the humiliations of the operation. Best of all, Kitty will not be able to scratch furniture or human skin, although she will be able to respond appropriately to bitchy remarks from other cats.

AC23098
Artificial Claws
Four Sets of Four Claws for Four Paws:
$29.95
(Glue Included)

CAT COLOGNES

THE SMELL YOU CAN'T FORGET

TIGER

For male cats only! With a drop of this on each flank your Tom will never need to spray again—every female in the neighborhood (human *or* feline) will be scratching after him. Recommended only for the most confident of young males—and this one is for outdoor cats *only*. Aunt Cora will *not* pay for repairs to windows, screen doors, or injuries "down there" that may result from using this **potent cologne.**

Tflkj58-92
Tiger Cologne
Per Ounce: $45

CHAT-EAU (also known as *Chat*-eau de Palm Springs)

Developed in Palm Springs, brewed in Antibes, and shipped **exclusively** to Aunt Cora, *Chat*-eau is so popular among cats that it's worn year-round. While intended for outdoor wear (its bouquet is distinctively strong and nearly permanent), housebound cats will find sunny days every night.

PX489098
Chat-eau
Per Ounce: $40

ALL NEW!

TABOO TABBÉ (Parfum de Paris)

Years ago Aunt Cora devised a perfume for long-haired cats only. Formerly, Aunt Cora allowed this secret aroma to be dispensed only in cat grooming salons, but now Taboo Tabbé can be a household indulgence for cats who remind you of Sophia Loren. Sleek, unforgettable, and **even a little naughty,** Taboo Tabbé should be used sparingly after a powder.

TT48902
Taboo Tabbé Parfum
Per Ounce: $190

MATERNITY WEAR

SALE!

FELINE MATERNITY OUTFITS

Why should Kitty sacrifice her glamour during those awkward weeks she endures before increasing the number of creatures that cat books can be written about? Kitty's prelabor days can be spent in high fashion, not looking like she washes the same old pillow case every night. Fourteen different designer outfits **cut to fit all sizes—** even the most ambitious pregnancies.

Feline Maternity Wear
Fourteen Outfits: $160.00

CAT TAGS

Aunt Cora is very concerned about the impending war in Central America and believes that every cat should be ready to serve his country. She has therefore begun designing combat uniforms for cats and has of course begun with the cat tag, a perfect replica of the famous dog tag that helped to identify so many of our soldiers in wars past. Not to be confused with a fashion item, these cat tags are patriotic emblems and will not be sold to **foreign breeds** (except Persians).

183912309812309
Cat Tags
(Includes your cat's draft registration and social security numbers, date of birth, and special allergies)
NOTE: Cat Tags are Free for a limited time only!

THE RAIN CHAPEAU

Very popular among the backyard cat set whose owners forget their responsibilities. Also for cats with a taste for ruined barbecues and water rats. Special attachment sticks easily to Kitty's head like a toupee. Also fits snugly on cats *with* toupees.

8709
A Feline Rain Chapeau
$10.95 Postpaid

NEW!

KITTY PANTY HOSE

Nothing keeps that feline shape younger and firmer than these specially designed panty hose. Revolutionary elastic keeps them up. **Teflon-reinforced to avoid embarrassing runs.** Available in all colors and in the following sizes: Siamese, Pekinese, Russian Blue, and Alley Gray.

87947 J
Kitty Hose
$3.95 Per Pair; Minimum Order: Six

CATTAILS

EXOTIC CAMOUFLAGE TAILS

Many a flock of peacocks have been unable to recognize Kitty in their midst—which enables Kitty to add a few more quills to her tail. Aunt Cora's Peacock Camouflage Tail can turn even a cat of mixed breed into a replica of the proudest bird of all—for hunting or decorative purposes.

And especially recommended for Persian or Siamese cats is Aunt Cora's brand-new *La Cage Aux Cats,* with the richest cluster of ostrich feathers imaginable. Only for the most outré of felines whose owners have a taste for the luxurious. As with all of Aunt Cora tails, special litter box accommodations must be arranged.

RUI 2748
Exotic Camouflage Tails
Peacock: $50
Ostrich: $75

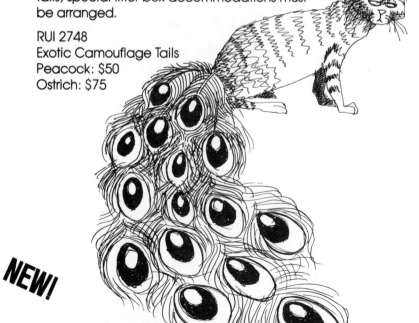

NEW!

CATTAILS

THE BEAVER LOOK

This is a disarmingly exciting new and natural look. Why not combine the best feline features with the best beaver feature? Utterly confuses the postman and the Avon lady. Allows Kitty to swat insects. (WARNING: Beaver look requires a special litter box if Kitty is to wear it regularly.)

BQ58093
The Beaver Look
Special: Only $30

SAVE!

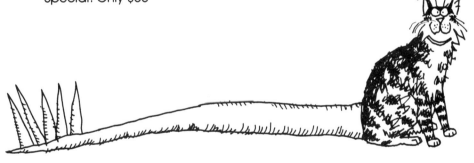

STEGASAURUS TAIL

Worried about the onset of a nuclear ice age? Don't. Kitty will be the first cat on your block to have the right look for the next dinosaur era. When ordering, state in which era you would like to receive the tail.

ST59083
STEGASAURUS TAIL
Small 3–5 Feet: $250.00
Medium 7–10 Feet: $300.00

UNUSUAL COLLARS

ALL NEW!

COLLARS FROM ENGLAND

Male cats will stun in the imported Prince Edward collar with a maroon striped tie. Everyone will take the instantly distinguished Mr. Kitty far more seriously. The tie is quite stiff to keep Kitty from tripping over it or dipping it into his food or water, and the collar is permanently starched.

But for female felines, Aunt Cora has gone all out in collaboration with the Tower of London gift shop to offer **authentic hand-made (no two are alike)** Elizabethan collars for especially regal kitties. Also makes a far more presentable alternative to the collars that Kitty's doctor gives her to keep her from biting her stitches. Guaranteed to astonish everyone in Kitty's presence. Who said a cat can't look like a king— or queen?

BF48093
Collars from England
a) Elizabeth: $142.00
b) Prince Edward: $39.00
One size fits all

NEHRU COLLAR

Now that Aunt Cora sees India emerging as a world power, she has made special arrangements with the Black Hole Boutique in Calcutta to import *authentic* Nehru collars for cats. **Not to be confused with the impossible collars that were popular in the sixties,** this is the real thing. Available in all neck sizes; all cotton.

NRH5785
Nehru Collar
Size: Thick
Thicker
Superthick
All $4.95 Postpaid

A KITTY FORM

Why shouldn't your cat's outfits be **as well-tailored as your own?** These ingeniously designed forms enable you to create Kitty's entire spring wardrobe without Kitty having to sit patiently while you accidentally stick pins into her potential donor organs. The "Cattiken" can be adjusted for those seasons when Kitty goes on a Tender Vittles binge but comes in three basic sizes: anorexic, middle-of-the-road, and fat cat.

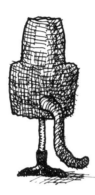

KF9804
Kitty Form
$89.95
Size: _____
Tail Length: _____

THE FELINE SLEEPING BAG

Now Kitty no longer need crawl inside your comforter on those cold winter nights. This sturdy sleeping bag was originally designed by members of a feminist collective in Vermont who didn't want male cats in bed with them. Because the bag is comfortable at temperatures as low as thirty degrees, it's ideal for camping trips. Not recommended for funerals. (NOTE: Next year Aunt Cora will introduce the Feline Electric Sleeping Bag with claw-proof cords.)

THXii38
FELINE SLEEPING BAG
Navy
$59.95

SALE!

THE GROUCHO MARX MAKE-OVER

The look that has amused **thousands of cat lovers!** Even Mel Brooks has had all of his cats altered to look like Groucho Marx—the Aunt Cora way. We'll fly Kitty to Rio de Janiero, where some of the best make-over plastic surgeons will alter Kitty's features to resemble the twentieth century's greatest comic. Imagine being able to say at dinner parties: "That's no cat, that's Groucho Marx!" Permanent cigar optional.

   (Next year Aunt Cora will introduce the Harpo Marx and Miss Piggy looks for Kitty.)

GM48903
$1,200
(Includes Flight, Three-Day Lodgings, Optional Cigar)

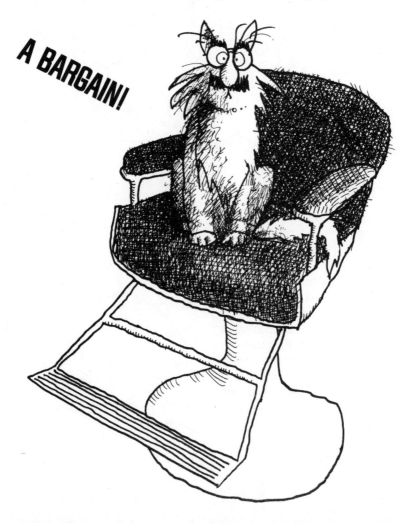

A BARGAIN!

ALL NEW!

AUNT CORA'S PARTY GAG: RUBBER CAT VOMIT

Nothing tickles a cat owner's funny bone like this sight gag. Gastro-enterologists at Kitty-Kettering Memorial Hospital were consulted to **assure the authenticity** of this *Animal House*-inspired trick. (Aunt Cora herself is known for her wicked sense of humor, but even she "tossed her cookies" over this one!) Just moisten the back and stick it to Madame's fur or muumuu. At first, she'll scream in horror, but years later the two of you can have the laughs and memories that mellow over the years.

DLJ4829
Rubber Cat Vomit
Special: $4.95

SPECIALTY STATIONERY

Convey those feline feelings through our new Catmark® card line. Cards for those special occasions: New Litter, Birthday, Get Well, Mother's Day, and Sympathy cards for altered or de-clawed cats.

CCR45789
Assortment of Twelve Cards with Envelopes:
$12
(NOTE: Inside illustrated card: "Sorry to hear about your claws.")

To a good friend......

BIRTH ANNOUNCEMENT CARDS

This box of twenty-four cards and envelopes is a must when that blessed event finally occurs. What better way to show your friends your position on abortion and birth control! Just send them out and get ready for all kinds of gifts of kitty litter and champagne. Box of twenty-four cards in pink or blue or twelve of each.

CKTRM
34567-K
Feline Birth Cards
Twenty-four and Envelopes $9.95

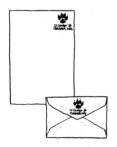

PERSONALIZED STATIONERY

Just send us Kitty's paw print (a pumpkin pie that Kitty has walked on will do) and Kitty's address, and we'll design a full set of aristocratic stationery that even the most elitist cats would be proud to scratch a line or two on and send off to those nearest and dearest. Only one color-blind shade of heavy cream. (A Helpful Little Note from Aunt Cora: "Yes, all kitties are color-blind.")

Sf77879
Set of Twenty-four Sheets and Matching Envelopes:
$15

THE FELINE FETISHIST'S CALENDAR

This is for the cat whose sensuality has become so specialized that only very specific body parts serve as aphrodisiacs. "March," for instance, stimulates Kitty with a tail. "April" is a single paw. "May" is a gaping nostril. "June" is . . . we can't reveal June, because, after all, Aunt Cora has always insisted that this is **a family catalog.**

XXX80489
Feline Fetishist Calendar
$15
(You must state that you are over twenty-one and that your cat is over four)

PENTMOUSE EROTIC CALENDAR

Keep your cat's sex life spicy with this **family-oriented** pornographic calendar. Our photographers have chosen some of the most desirable cats in Europe, and we've photographed them in sophisticated positions that will arouse even the stodgiest and grumpiest cat. Calendar is washable in case Kitty loses control.

Pentmouse Erotic Calendar
$18.95

NEW TITLES FOR THE FELINE LIBRARY

I LED NINE LIVES

Written by the cat owned by Sybil, this cat has so many personalities she sometimes trips over one of her other eight tails. *Publishers Weekly* called this **"The Big Cat Read of the Year."** Alternate selection of the Litter Guild.

BFKOpp272
I Led Nine Lives $13.95

SPECIAL!

THE NEW YORK EATING OUT GUIDE

This guide to the best garbage cans in New York City is a must for any cat who's passing through and wants to take a bite out of the Big Apple. **Lists all fish restaurants without tight security** and/or open garbage cans. Also comes with a fold-out map of Chinatown, which Kitty should probably avoid unless she wants to wind up as chop suey, according to Aunt Cora's sources.

48029849
Eating Out Guide $10.95

HOW MANY CATS DOES IT TAKE TO CHANGE A LIGHT BULB: A BOOK OF CAT HUMOR

A book of contemporary cat humor. This book will keep Kitty in Cheshire grins for days. Contains such jokes as: How can you tell the cat at the wedding? And: What did the traveling salesman say to the cat? And the ever popular: Why did the cat cross the road? **(Contains no dead kitten jokes.)**

40982398
Cat Humor $8.95

THE OFFICIAL I HATE CATS MORE THAN YOU DO BOOK!

Aunt Cora offers this anti-cat book only because she feels it is very important for America's cats to know who their enemies are. As Aunt Cora has said many times, "The price of the survival of the cat species is eternal vigilance."

BFKOpp282
I Hate Cats

LINGUISTIC SOFTWARE SPECIAL: INTRA-SPECIES LANGUAGE PROGRAMS

These software programs are the perfect answer to the problems Kitty has communicating with other animals. **Feline-friendly programs** are designed to give Kitty a full vocabulary in just fourteen days—all the skills necessary for talking in Pig, Cow, Goat, and Whale. Just take Kitty out into the country and she'll be the perfect interpreter. Next year, Aunt Cora will introduce her revolutionary new language: Human for Cats.

NP8077-3
Intra-Species Language Programs
$49 Per Language;
Two Languages for $80.

NEW VIDEOS FOR KITTY:

SPECIAL!

THE JANE FONDA WORKOUT FOR CATS

Work out with the woman who started it all!
Is Kitty beginning to look like a furry water barrel? Is
her double chin falling into her water dish? Can't
make it up on to the sofa in three jumps? Are your
friends telling you, "Oh, she's only putting on weight
because she was altered"? Well, Aunt Cora has
worked out **a special deal**: because Jane Fonda
is an old personal friend from Aunt Cora's old anti-
war days in Madison, Jane was only too happy to
provide a special work-out videotape for cats. Jane
purrs away the hour while Kitty purrs away the
pounds. And it's actually fun to watch Kitty getting
physically fit.

DPL4720
Jane Fonda Work-Out for Cats
(Specify Whether Beta or VHA Format)
$69.95

THE AUNT CORA WALK-CAT™

Everyone's tuning in and tuning out, so why shouldn't old four-paws get in the act? The Walk-Cat™ fits snugly on Kitty's delicate ears. Comes complete with tapes of some of Kitty's favorite sounds and music. *Scoobie—doo: Songs by Frank Sinatra's Cat* is a big favorite among Aunt Cora's brood. Kitty can also listen to hour-long tapes of the sounds that can openers make opening cans of tuna fish.

LMP3479
Aunt Cora Walk-Cat™
$69.95 (Batteries Not Included)

AUNT CORA'S GENETIC ENGINEERING KIT

Bored with two eyes and four paws? Aunt Cora's latest kit, with the most up-to-date DNA technology, will allow you to **tailor your next litter** of kittens to match your very own specifications. Why not add an extra eye or a fifth paw and **really** give the neighbors something to talk about? And you can crossbreed to develop a cat that doesn't eat because it is able to photosynthesize Tender Vittles just by sitting in the sun.

RNA459987
Genetic Engineering Kit
$19,350.00
(Special RNA Attachment:
$5,000 Extra)
(Additional Restriction Enzymes: $450)